PBL PLANNING GUIDE

A PLANNING, RESOURCE AND REFERENCE COMPANION TO THE INTRO TO PBL WORKSHOP

ENGAGEMENT, INNOVATION AND IMPACT BY DESIGN

PRINCIPAL AUTHOR:
Charity Allen

Produced by
PBL Consulting
936 NW 57th St
Seattle, WA 98107

Please contact
PBL Consulting at
www.pblconsulting.org,
360-440-3968 or
charity@pblconsulting.org
for more information.

GRAPHIC
DESIGN BY:
Charity Allen

PBL Planning Guide, 3rd Edition
Copyright © 2016 - PBL Consulting

www.pblconsulting.org

Mollie

DEEP LEARNING

LOVE OF LEARNING

EMPOWERMENT

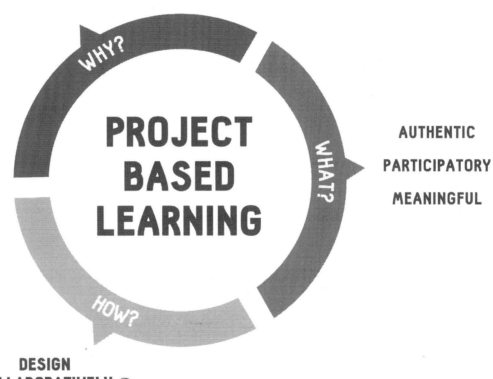

PROJECT BASED LEARNING

WHY?

WHAT?

HOW?

AUTHENTIC

PARTICIPATORY

MEANINGFUL

DESIGN COLLABORATIVELY

REFLECT & IMPROVE

IMPLEMENT FLEXIBLY

EXHIBIT PUBLICLY

PBL PLANNING GUIDE
TABLE OF CONTENTS

PBL PLANNING GUIDE
TABLE OF CONTENTS

HOW TO PLAN A PROJECT - PHASE TWO

HOW TO PLAN A PROJECT - PHASE THREE

HOW TO PLAN A PROJECT - PHASE FOUR

WORKSHOP IN A NUTSHELL

OBJECTIVES	To review and apply the project based learning design process. To develop a project-based experience to be implemented in your classroom.
DRIVING QUESTION	How can we develop effective and engaging project-based experiences for students?
MAJOR DELIVERABLES	• Gallery Walk Poster (showcasing initial project idea) • Project Alignment Guide • Project Calendar • Project in a Nutshell
ASSESSMENT	Nuts & Bolts Checklist Gallery Walk Protocol & Tuning Protocol
RESOURCES	Check out *www.pblconsulting.org*, *www.eleducation.org,* *www.hightechhigh.org*, *www.mathalicious.com*, *www.bie.org*, *www.nsrfharmony.org*, & *http://tinkering.exploratorium.edu/projects* for access to a wealth of PBL resources, protocols, project ideas, videos materials and more.

NOTES

CREATIVE DESIGN BRIEF

DRIVING QUESTION:
How can we develop effective and engaging project-based experiences for students?

CREATIVE CHALLENGE:
Develop a project that is effective and engaging that you can implement in your classroom.

IT SHOULD:
- Be engaging for students.
- Be engaging for you.
- Create a powerful context for learning – both academic learning outcomes and 21st century competencies, such as collaboration, critical thinking, communication, creativity and innovation.
- Incorporate the 9 Nuts and Bolts of PBL.
- Be implemented within 60 days. (*Recommended*)

TEAMS:
- Recommended: Pairs
- Optional: Triads
- Discouraged: Teams larger than 3

INSTRUCTIONS: Jot down your hopes and fears in response to your design challenge and the idea of doing project based learning in your classroom.

HOPES	FEARS

NEED TO KNOWS

What do I need to know to answer the Driving Question?

Driving Question: How can we design effective and engaging project based experiences for students?

NEED TO KNOWs	GOOD TO GOs	NEW NEED TO KNOWs
What I need to know, be able to do and/or understand to answer the Driving Question...	*Need to knows that you have addressed to your satisfaction.*	*Capture new, emerging need to knows here.*

PROJECTS VS. PBL

Consider projects you've seen and done over time as a leader, as a teacher and/or as a student. Were those "dessert projects" or real "main course project based learning" experiences?

INSTRUCTIONS: List the features of dessert projects and those of main course PBL below.

DESSERT	MAIN COURSE

Title: The Buzz on Bees
Grade Level(s): Grades 1-8 (Multi-age Classroom)
Type of Project: Design Challenge

Context:
A local beekeeper has noticed a decline in bee numbers and problems with pollination. Find out how big this problem is and its causes and effects

Driving Question:
How can we increase the number of pollinators available to our plants?

Learning Outcomes:
Small Flying & Crawling Creatures - Describe the relationships of pollinators to other living things in their habitat, and to people. Identify ways in which animals are considered helpful or harmful to humans and to the environment. Describe the relationships of these animals to other living and nonliving things in their habitat, and to people.

Plant Growth & Change - Identify and describe the general purpose of flowers. Describe life cycles of seed plants, and identify example methods used to ensure their germination, growth and reproduction describe the use of beehives to support pollination. Recognize that habitat preservation can help maintain animal populations and identify ways that student actions can assist habitat preservation.

Math - Data collection & graphing and other relevant learning outcomes to each grade level.

Writing for Purpose - Experiment with sentence patterns, imagery and exaggeration to create mood & mental images. Use repetition, rhyme and rhythm in shared language experiences, such as action songs and word play.

Presentation Skills

Tangible Outcomes:
  Products: A proposed change or device that could attract more bees.
  Performances: Poems or songs about bees.
  Presentation: Informational reading & writing

Adult World Connections:
  Interviews with beekeeper, gardener and/or field boss. Field work to count bees throughout process. Research data on bee numbers from research studies.

Authored and generously shared by
Calista Nielsen & Ken Hoekstra

Title: Lucy the Elephant
Grade: Kindergarten
Type of Project:
Problem Solving & Design Challenge

Context:
The Edmonton Zoo agreed to temporarily house a rescue elephant named Lucy. Unfortunately, the zoo doesn't have the space or facilities for keeping an elephant for the long-term. While they initially planned to transfer Lucy, they recently determined she is too sick and too old to withstand the move.

Learning Outcomes:
Animal habitats, reading informational texts, informational writing

Driving Question:
How can we redesign Lucy the Elephant's zoo enclosure so that she will be happy and comfortable?

Tangible Outcomes:
  Class: Habitat design idea
  Individual: Text / picture representation of an animal habitat (each student chooses an animal to feature)

Adult World Connections:
Zookeepers and field work at the zoo

Find these free sample projects at www.pblconsulting.org

Title: Seagull Squabble
Grade: 4th Grade
Type of Project: Controversial Issue

Context:
Students are challenged to propose a solution to the recent controversy in Elmira, New York: downtown business owners are putting pressure on the city council to limit the seagull population that nests on the islands in the Chemung River.

Driving Question:
How should we solve the seagull squabble?

Learning Outcomes:
3rd Grade Next Generation Science Standards: Ecosystems: Interactions, Energy, & Dynamics
3-LS2-1: Construct an argument that some animals form groups that help members survive.
3-LS2.D: Social Interactions and Group Behavior Being part of a group helps animals obtain food, defend themselves and cope with changes. Groups may serve different functions and vary dramatically in size.
CCSS Writing 3.1: Write opinion pieces on topics or texts, supporting a point of view with reasons.

Tangible Outcomes:
Team: Proposal to the city council (must have a presentational and a written component)
Individual: Position paper

Adult World Connections:
City council & local business owners involved on both sides of the issue.

Title: Biomimicry Designs
Grade: 1st Grade
Type of Project: Design Challenge

Context:
For years, humans have been stealing ideas from plants & animals to create tools, solve problems and enhance their lives. For example, the Baby Bjorn uses biomimicry of the kangaroo pouch. As teams of scientists and engineers, you will work together to examine multiple plants and animals as case studies for animal behavior, physical traits & human inspiration for biomimicry. Your challenge is to ideate and design a tool, inspired from nature, that helps humans.

Driving Question: What plant & animal traits could help us design a tool that helps humans?

Learning Outcomes:
1st Grade Next Generation Science Standards for Life Science
1-LS1-1: Use materials to design a solution to a human problem by mimicking how plants and/or animals use their external parts to help them survive, grow, & meet their needs.
1-LS1-2: Read texts and use media to determine patterns in behavior of parents and offspring that help offspring survive.
1-LS3-1: Make observations to construct an evidence-based account that young plants and animals are like, but not exactly like, their parents.
Crosscutting Concepts:(1) Structure and Function & (2) Patterns
Science and Engineering Practices: Constructing explanations and designing solutions.

Tangible Outcomes:
Individual: (1) "Case Study Journal" of multiple plants & animals regarding: (a) physical traits, (b) behaviors and (c) human inspiration for biomimicry. (2) Biomimicry Tool: Draft design, prototype and tool.
Class: "Biomimicry Case Study Chapter Book" (each student produces one page in the book that features the plant or animal that intrigued them the most.)
Team: Chapter introduction pages for the class book.

Adult World Connections:
REI / MEC gear experts and/or extreme adventurers, case studies from nature, observations in nature.

Title: Learniture
Grade: 7
Subject: Science
Type of Project: Design Challenge

Context:
You are tired of the used up 60s furniture that your parents have given you for your room. You will design and construct an original, stable, utilitarian and esthetically pleasing piece of furniture from up-cycled materials to use in your room.

Learning Outcomes:
Alberta Program of Studies:
Science: Structures / Forces
(1) Describe and interpret different types of structures encountered in everyday objects, buildings, plants and animals; and identify materials from which they are made.
(2) Investigate and analyze forces within structures, and forces applied to them.
(3) Investigate and analyze the properties of materials used in structures.
(4) Demonstrate and describe processes used in developing, evaluating and improving structures that will meet human needs with a margin of safety.

Driving Question:
How can you, as a budding furniture designer, design and build a usable piece of furniture for your room?

Tangible Outcomes:
Individual: Analysis of forces and types of structures. Explanation of why they selected the materials used. Students will investigate, analyze and share how their structure & materials would respond to applied forces.
Team: Finished furniture & presentation on process and planning. Students will describe the function and structural elements of their piece of furniture.

Adult World Connections:
Use of blueprints, graphic design software, visiting architects and designers.

Authored and generously shared by Sabrina Heydorn & Sheldon Nederlof

Title: A Fabulous Foray into French Fashion
Grade: 8
Subject: French I
Type of Project: Design Challenge

Context:
You are a fashion designer hoping to break into the market in Quebec. You must pitch your line and company via a design portfolio and promote your store or website using social media.

Learning Outcomes:
Written Production: Name, label, describe, ask & answer questions, express needs, desires, wishes and preferences, make suggestions.
Oral Production: Describe, explain, ask and answer questions.
Language: Vocabulary, adjectives, adverbs, interrogatives, sentence structure.
Culture: French search engines, implications of variations of French.
Language Learning Strategies: Cognates / word families, categorize info, anticipate info, tolerate ambiguity, take risks with texts, associate meanings with symbols.

Driving Question:
How can we break into the French fashion market in Quebec?

Tangible Outcomes:
Individual: A cohesive design portfolio (clothing & store/website), social media accounts, consumer surveys, a "pitch" presentation
Team: 2 portfolio pieces (clothing), 2 social media posts (post & comments), 2 occasions of consumer feedback, exercises/quizzes on sentence structure & adjective placement / agreement, plural construction / agreement.

Adult World Connections:
Review authentic portfolios and authentic products in French, interview experts, conduct focus groups.

Authored and generously shared by An Nguyen

Title: Food for Thought
Grade: 6
Subject: English Language Arts
Type of Project: Problem Solving

Context:
There is an abundant amount of food wasted nationally in the United States every day. Furthermore, locally in our own school our school administration, during their daily monitoring of cafeteria footage, has noticed a high amount of food wasted by students. They wonder if this is a common problem in schools across the United States, and beyond. They have decided to task the students with identifying the severity of this problem and developing possible solutions to reduce food waste at a school, local and/or national level.

Learning Outcomes:
CCSS - Citing textual evidence, determining a central idea, evaluating arguments and claims, presenting claims and findings, adapting speech to fit audience

Driving Question:
What are the best ways to take action to reduce food waste in our school and beyond?

Tangible Outcomes:
Individual: (1) Generated questions for inquiry and research inspired by Driving Question; (2) Pictograph representing data found during research process supporting need for a solution
Team: (1) Reflection on results of research driven by generated questions; (2) Choice of solution action plan; (3) Creation of an artifact representative of the solution; (4) Presentation to stakeholders of questions, research, reflection, solution and artifact.

Adult World Connections:
District Food Service Director, food bank representative, local restaurant owner, waste/landfill owner

Title: Teen Tragedy
Subject: English Language Arts
Grade: 10
Type of Project: Controversial Issue

Context:
Recently in Dallas, Texas, several teenagers were hanging out at a subway stop. Allegedly, one boy tried to steal the mp3 device of another boy in a group. A fight broke out and one boy was pushed into the subway tracks and was inadvertently killed by an oncoming train. The boy who pushed the deceased teenager is on trial for manslaughter. The prosecution is petitioning to have him tried as an adult. Winning this petition would open the door to the possibility of the death penalty or life in prison if he is found guilty.

Learning Outcomes:
Persuasive writing, writing for purpose, research, taking perspectives, taking a position, thesis statement writing, topic sentences, organization of writing, the writing process.

Driving Question:
How can I influence stakeholders in the Dallas teen tragedy?

Tangible Outcomes:
Individual: Options: Letter to the editor, letter to the judge, letter to the defense team, letter to the prosecution, blog, etc.
Team: Case study analysis presentations (during the project.)

Adult World Connections:
Lawyers, authentic legal precedent cases.

Find these free sample projects at www.pblconsulting.org

Title: Tsunami Warnings
Subject: Math: Trigonometry
Type of Project: Design Challenge

Context:

Ocean buoys have been developed as a predictor of catastrophic wave action. Many buoys around the world's oceans use outdated technology and provide insufficient detection and therefore warning. When an earthquake happens, it can move the water around it enough to cause large waves and move forward until it hits the coast. We use sine and cosine to measure the length of waves, which can be used to figure out how fast a tsunami is going in order to warn people in time. Technology could also be used to measure and to record tsunamis. Students will research tsunami buoy systems now in place to gather data, predict the trigonometric function (sine) used to analyze waves, including amplitude and fundamental period.

Learning Outcomes:

CCSS.Math - HSF.TF.B.5 - Choose trigonometric functions to model periodic phenomena with specified amplitude, frequency, and midline.
CCSS.Math - HSF.TF.B.7 - Use inverse functions to solve trigonometric equations that arise in modeling contexts; evaluate the solutions using technology, & interpret them in terms of the context
Collaboration Skills

Driving Question:

How can we develop a mathematically sound model to predict tsunamis in countries currently unprotected?

Tangible Outcomes:

Individual: Flow charts & graphs of data-driven sine curves
Team: Tsunami protection algorithm
Class: Blog

Adult World Connections:

Collection, review and analysis of primary data from tsunami detection organizations and databases

Title: Elemental Applications
Subject: Chemistry
Type of Project: Design Challenge

Context:

Several schools have created apps that have hit the top ten lists. Students will respond to a design challenge and create an app, similar to the Akinator app, which can accurately guess any element on the Periodic Table.

Learning Outcomes:

NGSS - HS-PS1-1: Use the periodic table as a model to predict the relative properties of elements based on the patterns of electrons in the outermost energy level of atoms.
NGSS - PS1.A: (1) Structure and properties of matter, (2) structure and interactions of matter and (3) organization of and patterns on the periodic table, such as the arrangement of the periodic table based on electron filling orders, and periodic trends: atomic radius, ionic radius, ionization energy, electron affinities and electronegativities.

Driving Question:

How can I design an app that can accurately guess any element on the periodic table, that people actually want to download?

Tangible Outcomes:

Individual: Questioning flow charts, mini-presentations on 1-2 elements, quizzes
Team: App questioning flow charts & optional application

Adult World Connections:

App designers work with students during the project & use of "Akinator" app as model.

Find these free sample projects at www.pblconsulting.org

14

Title: The Nuremburg Trials
Subject: World History
Type of Project: Simulation

Context:
Set in Nazi Germany, students are asked to take on the role of expert witness and to develop testimony from one of four different perspectives (Jewish person, German soldier, high-ranking German government official & journalists from various European countries) for the Nuremberg Trial.

Driving Question:
How can I present and defend my point of view of the Holocaust as a witness testifying at the Nuremberg Trials?

Learning Outcomes:
C3 SS Framework - D2.His.4.9-12 - Analyze complex and interacting factors that influenced the perspectives of people during different historical eras.
C3 - D2.His.16.9-12 - Integrate evidence from multiple relevant historical sources & interpretations into a reasoned argument about the past.
C3 - D4.4.9-12 - Critique the use of claims and evidence in arguments for credibility.
C3 - D4.5.9-12 - Critique the use of the reasoning, sequencing and supporting details of explanations.
Presentation Skills

Tangible Outcomes:
Individual: (1) Expert testimony (written), (2) source critique and (3) WWII key player character profiles (presentations during project)
Team: (1) Perspective presentations (during project), (2) interview questions and (3) oral expert testimony
Class: Mock Trial (trial simulation)

Adult World Connections:
Interview of veterans, historians or survivors. Volunteer lawyers supporting mock trial. Primary sources.

Title: ZAP Project
Subject: ELA / Social Studies: Geography
Type of Project: Scenario

Context:
Zombie apocalypse scenario in which students are tasked with a mission from the CDC to develop radio broadcasts and tools to maximize human survival in the face of the spreading virus.

Learning Outcomes:
Geography - (1) Understand the use of geographic tools to locate and analyze information about people, places and environments. (2) Understand how human factors & the distribution of resources affect the development of society & the movement of populations. (3) Understand how cultural factors influence the design of human communities. (4) Understand people create places that reflect culture, human needs, government policy and current values & ideals as they design & build places.

Driving Question:
How can we help humans survive the spreading zombie virus and create safe, uninfected and sustainable new human communities?

Tangible Outcomes:
Individual: Radio script segments, settlement position paper & outbreak update map
Team: Emergency radio broadcasts, new settlement blueprint & outbreak origin map

Adult World Connections:
Radio broadcast developers and community leaders work with students throughout the project. CDC data on flu epidemics as well as Census Bureau data on population trends.

(See more on this project in the Sample Projects section)

NINE NUTS & BOLTS OF PBL

1. **Academic Learning Outcomes**

2. **21st Century Competencies**

3. **Tangible Outcomes**
   Products, Performances, Presentations and/or Services

4. **Focused Inquiry**

5. **Focusing Question(s)**

6. **Engaging Context**

7. **Student Voice & Choice**

8. **Drafting & Critique**

9. **Adult World Connections**

Project Based Learning is a methodology of teaching and learning in which students respond to real-world challenges, problems, controversies, scenarios and simulations through a process of focused, student-influenced inquiry with the goals of:

1. genuine student engagement
2. mastery of academic learning outcomes
3. development of 21st century competencies
4. production of tangible outcomes

END IN MIND

Mastery of Academic Learning Outcomes	Development of 21st Century Competencies	Creation of Tangible Outcomes Products, Performances, Presentations & Services

MEANS TO THE END

Focused Inquiry	Focusing Question(s)	Engaging Context	Student Voice & Choice	Drafting & Critique	Adult World Connections

CLASSIFICATION LEVEL: SECRET
MEMORANDUM FOR Special Task Force NATCOMM
SUBJECT: National Emergency Communications

TASK: Due to a lethal and violent virus rapidly spreading across the globe, you are being tasked with a world-saving mission. As radio broadcasters, your team will develop a series of emergency radio broadcasts and accompanying tools to maximize potential human survival. You will need to draw from your knowledge, access a variety of resources and work with experts to build understanding of:
- Using & Creating Geographic Tools
- Distribution, Movement and Characteristics of Human Populations
- Interdependence of People, Places and Environments
- Distribution of Resources as well as Resource Management
- Human Society, Culture and Communities

BACKGROUND: The data indicates that the outbreak originated in Dallas, Texas and quickly spread through car and air commuter routes. Infection rates are rising exponentially. We will send more data to inform your work in subsequent communications.

DELIVERABLES:
- **Emergency Radio Broadcasts**
  These are intended to update uninfected humans with survival recommendations and access points for tools and resources.
- **Origin Outbreak Map**
  Please include writing on anticipated spread routes based on your analysis of geography, historic migration and current population patterns.
- **Map Series – Outbreak Updates**
  Must include directional escape routes and safe zones, this should be a series that is kept up to date to represent quickly changing conditions.
- **New Settlement Blueprints**
  Must include laws, governance structure and/or social contract as well as guidelines for resource management.

The fate of human survival rests in your hands. Good luck!

Find this free sample project at www.pblconsulting.org

PROJECT IN A NUTSHELL

PROJECT IN A NUTSHELL

Project Title: ZAP ~ Zombie Apocalypse Preparedness	Estimated Length: 4 weeks
Subject(s): ELA / Social Studies - Geography	Grade Level(s): 9th grade

LEARNING OUTCOMES

Academic Learning Outcomes	21st Century Competencies
Geography - (1) Understand the use of geographic tools to locate and analyze information about people, places & environments. (2) Understand how human factors & the distribution of resources affect the development of society & the movement of populations. (3) Understand how cultural factors influence the design of human communities. (4) Understand people create places that reflect culture, human needs, government policy, and current values and ideals as they design & build places. Writing for Purpose. Speaking & Listening.	☑ **Collaboration** ☐ Presentation ☐ Creativity & Innovation ☐ Critical Thinking ☐ Other:

ENGAGING CONTEXT

Type of project	Summary of the challenge, problem, controversy, issue, simulation
☐ Design challenge / ☐ Tribute work ☐ Problem solving ☐ Addressing a controversial issue ☐ Addressing a local / national / intl issue ☑ **Simulation or scenario** ☐ Other:	Zombie apocalypse scenario in which students are tasked with a mission from the CDC to develop radio broadcasts and tools to maximize human survival in the face of the spreading virus.

FOCUSED INQUIRY

Focusing Question(s)	Method of inquiry to be used	Tools needed
How can we help humans survive the spreading zombie virus and create safe, uninfected and sustainable new human communities?	☐ Engineering Design Process ☐ Design Thinking ☐ Problem Solving Process ☐ Scientific Method ☑ **Open Ended Inquiry** ☐ Decision Making Process ☐ Historical Method ☐ Other:	☐ Inquiry Journals ☐ Reflection Prompts ☐ Observation ☑ **Authentic Documents** ☐ Primary Data ☐ Field Work ☑ **Adults Outside of School** ☐ Other:

TANGIBLE OUTCOMES: PRODUCTS, PERFORMANCES, PRESENTATIONS & SERVICES

Individual	Team	Class
1. Outbreak Origin Map 2. Radio Broadcasts 3. New Settlement Blueprint	1. Outbreak Update Map 2. Radio Script Segment 3. Settlement Position Paper	n/a

ADULT WORLD CONNECTIONS

Authentic documents, data, samples, models, etc.	Professionals, stakeholders, organizations, experts, etc.	Primary research, field work, observation, experimentation
CDC Data on Flu Epidemics Census Bureau Data on Population NPR podcast & new broadcast samples Case Studies on Human Communities	Radio broadcast professionals to support development of high quality radio productions Community leaders to be used as a resource for information on the structure of community & management of nat. resources.	n/a

ZAP PROJECT – 9TH GRADE
PROJECT ALIGNMENT GUIDE

PROJECT ALIGNMENT GUIDE

TANGIBLE OUTCOMES: Products, performances, presentations & services	LEARNING OUTCOMES: Aligned to tangible outcomes	INSTRUCTION: Lessons, workshops, materials, resources, demos, scaffolding, protocols, modeling, media, etc.	FORMATIVE ASSESSMENTS: Critiques, drafting, rehearsals & progress checks to be conducted during the project
Radio Script Segments (individual) Radio Broadcast (team)	Geography - Understand how human factors & the distribution of resources affect the development of society & the movement of populations.	Activity: Population map series analysis Guided Reading: Textbook section & US Census Bureau data on population Video: Excerpts from several documentaries on population growth and change Text Based Discussion Protocol "Say Something:" CDC data on flu epidemics & textbook section on natural disasters	Post-video questions Post-discussion debriefs Reflection questions Questions for understanding
	Radio Production Writing for purpose Speaking & Listening	Demo: Expert visit Student-led lesson: Using Audacity to record. Writers' workshops series: Writing & production Critique models: NPR podcasts and news segments - "This American Life," "Invisibilia" and "Fresh Air"	Draft scripts Oral rehearsals Draft recordings Peer & expert critique sessions of drafts (rotational critique protocol)
Outbreak Origin Map (team) Outbreak Update Maps (indv)	Geography - Understand the use of geographic tools to locate and analyze information about people, places and environments.	Instructional Critique: Industry map samples shared & critiqued as a lesson Inquiry centers: with various types of maps to show map features, styles and scales for collaborative discussion On-demand mini-lessons	"Gallery Walk Protocol" of map drafts
	Collaboration Skills	Self & Team Assessments: Team contract template, BIE collaboration rubric, prompts for reflection in collaboration journal Mini-Lesson: Setting SMART Goals	Deliverable: Team contract with collaboration norms (team deliverable) Deliverable: Individual collaboration journals Deliverable: SMART Goals (individual)
Settlement 5 paragraph Position Paper (indv.) New Settlement Blueprint (team)	Geography - Understand how cultural factors influence the design of human communities.	Mini-lesson: Functions, services, land and patterns of settlement. Independent research based on NTKs	Individual Papers: "Gallery Walk Protocol" of thesis statements and topic sentences and pair critique
	Geography - Understand people create places that reflect culture, human needs, government policy and current values & ideals as they design & build places.	Socratic Seminar: Two international case studies on human communities (Student-led Socratic Sem. facilitators) 5 paragraph position paper template Instructional critique: Persuasive writing Expert Visit: Q & A on local community resource management	Blueprints: Team A/B critique protocol Post-SS Debriefs Exit Tickets

PROJECT CALENDAR

Project Title: ZAP	Focusing Question: How can we help humans survive the spreading zombie virus and create safe, uninfected and sustainable new human communities?

WEEK ONE

Focus of the week: Geography: Maps, tools and technologies.

Entry Event: Letter from CDC Need-to-Know List Project teams announced First Team Meeting: Team Contract & collaboration norms due	Explanation of project details and rubrics Assessment: Sample radio broadcasts (using rubric) Team Meeting: Update NTKs and initial task list HW: Textbook section on maps. Read and respond to questions.	CDC Update Communication – CDC data on flu epidemics Team Work Time: Outbreak Origin Maps Gallery Walk Protocol Team Meeting: Sign up for mini-workshops or create work plan for Thurs./Fri.	Mini-workshop: Teacher facilitated on maps, tools and technologies Team Work Time: Revise Outbreak Origin Maps Team Meeting: Evaluate NTKs, task list and workshop selection	Quiz 1 – Geographical tools Mini-workshop: Teacher facilitated on forms of government Team meeting: Team and individual collaboration assessment

WEEK TWO

Focus of the week: Human communities, settlement blueprints & individual papers

CDC Update Communication – Outbreak Spread Update & Data Sets – Individual Update Map Assignments Given HW: Read case studies for Socratic Seminar	Socratic Seminar – resource management case studies Team check-in: Reassess task list & review Need-to-know list HW: Craft questions for tomorrow's expert visit	Individual Update Map Assignments Due Expert visit: Q & A on local community resource management (30 mins) Team meeting: Work plan or sign up for workshops HW: Documentary excerpts	Mini-workshop: Teacher facilitated on settlements Individual Work Time (Settlement paper thesis) Team meeting: Reassess task list HW: Team determined	Mini-workshop: Teacher facilitated on settlements Individual Work Time (Settlement paper outline) "Gallery Walk" protocol Mini-Workshop: SMART goal setting. Collaboration self-assessment & goal setting using template

WEEK THREE

Focus of the week: Radio Productions, Individual Papers Due Wednesday

Mini-workshop: Expert facilitated - writing radio scripts Team Work Time: (Radio Scripts) Team Check-in: Task list	Critique: "A / B teams" review radio scripts Mini-workshop: Expert facilitated - producing a radio broadcast Team Work Time: Radio Broadcast Production (draft)	Individual Settlement Papers Due Critique: Experts working with teams to critique and revise radio broadcasts Check-in: Your need-to-know lists	Team Work Time: (Settlement Blueprints) (Broadcast Production) Team Meeting: Sign up for last minute mini-workshops or create work plan for Friday	Mini-workshop: Teacher facilitated based on latest need-to-know list Work Time: (Team Determined) Team Meeting: Team and individual collaboration assessments

WEEK FOUR

Focus of the week: Settlement Blueprints & Presentation Prep

Team Work Time: (Settlement Blueprints) Team Meeting: Final task list HW: Team determined	Critique: Experts working with teams to critique and revise blueprints Team Work Time: (Settlement Blueprints) (Broadcast Production) HW: Team determined	Team Work Time: (Settlement Blueprints) (Broadcast Production) (Presentation Day Prep) HW: Team determined	Station Style Presentations "Open House"	Debrief & reflection Final Assessment: Self and peer collaboration Celebration!!

THRIVE
PUBLIC SCHOOLS

The Story of the Stars

Description:

The Story of the Stars will be an opportunity for students to develop an understanding of stars & astronomy from the history of the discipline to everyday sciences, as well as the power and the art of storytelling & mythology. Daily lessons will be built around student wonderings and essential skills. Some of the work that students will do will range from individuals, to groups, to working with families on a weekly blog entry. To become experts we will learn from a variety of experts from San Diego Astronomy Association to expert story tellers.

Driving question: What roles do stars have in our universe?

Essential Learning Skills:

NUMERACY	LITERACY
• Count, order, name, and write numbers to 20 • Comparing and grouping • 2-D Shapes • Calendar components	• Components of a book • Letter recognition & sounds • Blend and segmenting sounds • Write about things I know • Speak and share my ideas
SCIENCE & SOCIAL STUDIES	TINKERING
• Greek & Native American star stories • The tradition of oral storytelling • Day and night sky • Space systems	• Principles of Electricity • Circuitry

Final products for presentations of learning:
- Student created constellation LED sewn circuit art
- Created constellation myth
- Class collaboration constellation primary reader
- Inquiry journal

Experts and Fieldwork:
- Stars in the Park, SDAA
- Reuben H. Fleet Center
- Story Pirates
- Linda White, professional storyteller

How to help:

We are so grateful for all the wonderful assistance we had during our last project and are hoping for the same as we take our journey through space. During this project, we will be holding a parent meeting to discuss different volunteer opportunities in the classroom. We would appreciate any empty and cleaned food cans, that can be brought in whenever possible. Our goal is to also go on a fieldwork excursion or two during this project and volunteers will be an absolute must!
Please watch your email, website or handouts for communications about these opportunities.
If you have any connections or resources to donate, we would greatly appreciate your donation around these topics, thanks!

*Check out our Digital Portfolio for more information and extension resources!

Find this free sample project at www.pblconsulting.org

THE STORY OF THE STARS

PROJECT IN A NUTSHELL

PROJECT IN A NUTSHELL

Project Title: The Story of the Stars	Estimated Length: 8 weeks
Subject(s): Literacy, numeracy, sciences & tinkering	Grade Level(s): PreK - Kindergarten multi-age

LEARNING OUTCOMES

Academic Learning Outcomes	21st Century Competencies
Literacy: (1) Identify characters, setting and major events in a story. (2) Draw & write to narrate a single event or several loosely linked events. (3) Drawing & write to compose informative/explanatory text Numeracy: (1) Number and counting in sequence. (2) Compare numbers & objects. (3) Describe and compare measurable attributes. Sciences: Stars and space Tinkering: Principles of electricity and circuitry	☐ Collaboration ☐ Presentation ☑ **Creativity & Innovation** ☐ Critical Thinking ☐ Other:

ENGAGING CONTEXT

Type of project	Summary of the challenge, problem, controversy, issue, simulation
☑ **Design challenge** ☐ Tribute work ☐ Problem solving ☐ Addressing a controversial issue ☐ Addressing a local / nat / intl issue ☐ Simulation or scenario ☑ **Other:** Acting as an astronomer	Junior astronomers will dive into the universe of stars and space through the lens of story tellers. Day to day learning objectives will build knowledge about the science and the significance of stars & common constellations. Astronomers will observe, document and explore the stars in conjunction with the process and art of storytelling & recording in order to synthesize the different roles of stars in our universe.

FOCUSED INQUIRY

Focusing Question(s)	Method of inquiry to be used	Tools needed
What roles do stars have in our universe?	☐ Engineering Design Process ☐ Design Thinking ☐ Problem Solving Process ☐ Scientific Method ☑ **Open Ended Inquiry** ☐ Decision Making Process ☐ Historical Method ☐ Other:	☑ **Inquiry Journals** ☑ **Reflection Prompts** ☑ **Observation** ☐ Authentic Documents ☑ **Primary Data** ☑ **Field Work** ☑ **Adults Outside of School** ☐ Other:

TANGIBLE OUTCOMES: PRODUCTS, PERFORMANCES, PRESENTATIONS & SERVICES

Individual	Class
1. Stars & space inquiry journal 2. Created constellation, constellation character & creation myth 3. LED circuit art piece of their created constellation 4. Oral presentation of original constellation myth	Class constructed "Just Right" style early reader called, The Constellations We Know

ADULT WORLD CONNECTIONS

Authentic documents, data, samples, models, etc.	Organizations, experts stakeholders, etc.	Primary research, field work, observation, experimentation, etc.
Adopt and name a star Star maps	Stars in the Park with the San Diego Astronomy Association. Diane White: professional story teller Story Pirates, professional story tellers	Ruben H. Fleet Science Center: The Sky Tonight planetarium San Diego Observatory

THE STORY OF THE STARS
PROJECT ALIGNMENT GUIDE

PROJECT ALIGNMENT GUIDE			
TANGIBLE OUTCOMES: Products, performances, presentations & services	**LEARNING OUTCOMES:** Aligned to tangible outcomes	**INSTRUCTION:** Lessons, workshops, materials, resources, demos, scaffolding, protocols, modeling, media, etc.	**FORMATIVE ASSESSMENTS:** Critiques, drafting, rehearsals & progress checks to be conducted during the project
Stars & space inquiry journal	CCSS W.K.2 - Drawing & write to compose informative/ explanatory text	**Science lessons:** Student observations on books, videos, discussions and other resources on major space systems **Writer's workshops:** Informative writing about wonderings on stars & space	- Match the name to the stars - Written reflection in inquiry journal - Weekly blog posts - Writer's workshop journal - Weekly blog posts
	CCSS W.K.8 - With guidance & support from adults, recall information from experiences or gather info from provided sources to answer a question.	**Reader's workshops:** Read and explore the well-known myths around stars (The Big & Little Dipper, Ursa Major, Taurus, Cygnus, Orion, Pegasus, Canis Major, Serpens Kaput)	- Partner retell texts - Balanced literacy centers - Reflection prompts
	Space systems	**Science Lessons:** Space systems (Student-driven, based on student interest, questions and wonders...)	- Constellation puzzles - Constellation rock formations - Constellation connect the dots - Exit slips
Created constellation, character & creation myth	CCSS RL.K.3 - Identify characters, setting and major events in a story	**Reader's workshops:** Read and explore the well known myths around stars (The Big & Little Dipper, Ursa Major, Taurus, Cygnus, Orion, Pegasus, Canis Major, Serpens Kaput)	- Story retelling - Character "tell-alls" - Balanced literacy centers - Reflection prompts
	CCSS.RL.K.2 - Draw & write to narrate a single event or several loosely linked events	**Writer's workshops:** Character creation, what makes a myth, narrative writings with constellation as main character	- Peer share, peer critique, teacher critique, class created rubric
		Reader's workshops: 5 parts of a story (characters, setting, beginning, middle & end)	- Retell texts - Reflection prompts
		Art Lessons: Scientific drawings, tracing drafts, connecting words w/ illustrations	- Drafting and critique sessions - Class created rubric
Class constructed "Just Right" early reader called: The Constellations We Know	CCSS.W.K.2 - Drawing & write to compose informative/ explanatory text	**Science lessons:** Student observations on books, videos, discussions and other resources on space systems	- Constellation observation pages - Written reflection in inquiry journal
	Number and counting in sequence & describe and compare measurable attributes	**Math lessons:** How many stars are in the constellations we are studying?	- Math Centers - Counting practices & games - Blended adaptive math program
LED circuit art of their original constellation	Use tools and materials to build and light a circuit	**Tinkering workshops:** Circuits, electricity, tool safety	- Circuit testing - Tracing samples - Constellation connect the dots - Stars placement page
Oral presentation of created constellation myth	Presentation of Knowledge and Ideas: CCSS - ELA - LITERACY: SL.K.4 - Describe familiar people, places, things, and events and, with prompting and support, provide additional detail. SL.K.5 - Add drawings or other visual displays to descriptions as desired to provide additional detail. SL.K.6 - Speak audibly & express thoughts, feelings, & ideas clearly	**Exhibition practice:** Review presentation learning targets, watch & critique sample presentations (good and bad.)	- Exhibition practice: practice, observe and critique student presentations. - Exhibition set up & rehearsals - Exhibition !

THE STORY OF THE STARS
PROJECT CALENDAR

PROJECT CALENDAR

Project Title: The Story of the Stars | **Focusing Question:** What role do stars have in our universe?

WEEK ONE

Focus of the week: Kick off and build background knowledge

Launch Event: Act out the Apple Star Myth as a reader's theatre **Pre-assessment:** What do you already know about space? Stars and space wondering wall **Art Project:** My name in the stars	**Science:** What is a star? **Literacy:** read aloud, The North Star **Art:** How to draw a star shape with a connect the dots.	**Science:** What is the life cycle of a star?: Our Sun, BrainPop Jr. 'Sun" Video **Literacy:** read aloud, Stars **Math:** Connect the stars sequencing numbers **Tinkering:** What is electricity?	**Science:** What is the life cycle of a star? Supernovas & black holes **Literacy:** Leveled life cycle readers **Art:** Supernova water color	**Science:** Who studies stars? How did they study stars long ago? **Literacy:** Read aloud on Galileo **Math:** Connect the stars sequencing numbers **Tinkering:** What is an electron? **Weekly blog post:** I know that stars...

WEEK TWO

Focus of the week: Build on background knowledge of stars and begin talking about circuits.

Science: Who are the important astronomers & what did they discover? **Literacy:** Read aloud on Newton & gravity **Tinkering:** The history behind the science of electricity.	**Science:** What do astronomers use to study the stars? **Literacy:** Nonfiction reading on telescopes **Art:** Build our own telescopes	**Science:** The Hubble Space Telescope **Field Work:** San Diego Reuben H. Fleet Center **Literacy:** What is a myth?	**Science:** What is the Milky way? **Literacy:** What is a myth? Read aloud: How the stars came to be **Tinkering:** What is static electricity? **Art:** Make Galaxy Goo	**Science:** What is our cosmic address? **Math:** Ordering and comparing star sizes **Tinkering:** What is current electricity? **Weekly blog post:** Build and name your own constellation

WEEK THREE

Focus of the week: What is a constellation?

What is a constellation?	Ursa Major	Taurus	Pegasus	Cygnus
Science: Where in the sky is the Big dipper? What stars compose the constellation? **Literacy:** The story of the big dipper & the North Star **Numeracy:** Recreate constellation and count the stars **Tinkering:** How do we make electricity?	**Science:** Where in the sky is Ursa Major? What stars compose the constellation? **Literacy:** The story of Ursa Major & Ursa Minor **Writing:** How can you relate to Ursa Major's myth? **Numeracy:** Recreate constellation and count the stars **Art:** Constellation flashlight disc & sewing practice	**Science:** Where in the sky is Taurus? What stars compose the constellation? **Literacy:** The story of the big Taurus **Writing:** How do you feel about what Tarus did in his Myth? **Numeracy:** Recreate constellation and count the stars **Art:** Constellation flashlight disc & sewing practice	**Science:** Where in the sky is Pegasus? What stars compose the constellation? **Literacy:** The story of the Pegasus **Writing:** If you could use Pegasus to fly you anywhere where would he take you? **Numeracy:** Recreate constellation and count the stars **Art:** Constellation flashlight disc & sewing practice	**Science:** Where in the sky is the Cygnus? What stars compose the constellation? **Literacy:** The story of Cygnus **Writing:** Knowing Cygnus' myth, what does it mean to be loyal and a true friend? **Numeracy:** Recreate constellation and count the stars **Art:** Constellation flashlight disc & sewing practice **Blog post:** What constellation story have you connected with most?

THE STORY OF THE STARS
PROJECT CALENDAR

WEEK FOUR

Focus of the week: Mastering constellations & begin writing book

Canis Major

- Science: Where in the sky is Canis Major? What stars compose the constellation?

- Literacy: The story of Canis Major

- Writing: If you could use Pegasus to fly anywhere, where would he take you?

- Numeracy: Recreate constellation and count the stars

Art: Constellation flashlight disc & sewing practice

Serpens Caput

- Science: Where in the sky is Serpens Caput? What stars compose the constellation?

- Literacy: The story of Serpens Caput

- Writing: The serpent is a symbol for medicine, tell about a time you acted like a doctor.

- Numeracy: Recreate constellation & count the stars

Art: Constellation flashlight disc & sewing practice

Orion

Science: Where in the sky is Canis Major? What stars compose the constellation?

Literacy: The story of Canis Major

Writing: If you could use Pegasus to fly you anywhere where would he take you?

Numeracy: Recreate constellation and count the stars

Art: Constellation flashlight disc & sewing practice

Field Work: Stars in the park with SD Astronomy Association (7pm)

Constellation recap

Science: Revisit "wondering wall."

What have we answered what new wonderings do we now have?

Writing: In mastery groups, begin drafting book pages

Math: Compare the constellations

Tinkering: What is a battery?

The North Star

Science: The importance of North Star

Literacy: The history of oral storytelling

Writing: Continue to draft and revise book pages.

Tinkering: How do you make an electromagnet?

Blog post: Go stargazing tonight and tell us what you see.

WEEK FIVE

Focus of the week: Oral storytelling & character development

Science: Our expanding universe...

Literacy: The art of telling oral stories

Tinkering: Safety with electricity

Science: What is a shooting star?

Literacy: Practice retelling the "3 Farming Brothers" story

Art: Make a shooting star and dance the Shooting star dance

Science: Why do stars twinkle?

Literacy: Expert visit: The Story Pirates come to visit & share.

Tinkering: What is a circuit?

Science: Why do we only see stars at night?

Literacy: Character development

Art: Find and trace your character using transparent paper

Science: What is the difference between a star & a planet?

Literacy: Character develop. partner share

Tinkering: What is an open circuit? What is a closed circuit?

Blog post: If you were to go on a space mission, what would you bring with you?

WEEK SIX

Focus of the week: Story development

Literacy: Myth study, How the Stars Fell into the Sky

Writing: Story develop. How to start. What happens at the beginning of your story?

Tinkering: What is a parallel circuit?

Literacy: Myth study: They Dance in the Sky

Writing: Draft and revise story beginnings

Tinkering: Series circuits

Art: Draft a detailed illustration of your constellation character

Literacy: Myth Study: Korean Children's Favorite Stories

Writing: What makes a strong middle?

Tinkering: Build potato circuits

Literacy: Myth study: Turquoise Boy

Writing: Revise and draft middle of constellation myth

Tinkering: Make canvas for circuit art & transfer star pattern

Art: Continue to draft constellation character illustration

Literacy: What makes a strong oral story?

Writing: What makes a strong ending to a story?

Tinkering: Lay copper wire, label positive/negative track

Blog post: Write a myth about how stars came about.

WEEK SEVEN

Focus of the week: Publish constellation myth, finalize LED art piece

Literacy: How to retell a story with vocal expression **Writing:** Revise and draft end of constellation myth **Tinkering:** Prep & add LED lights.	**Expert:** Linda White, professional story teller. Share tips and critique student work **Writing:** Revise & draft constellation myths **Tinkering:** Connect lights and add final touches	**Literacy:** How to tell a story with your body **Writing:** Final drafts and publishing story **Art:** Final draft of character illustration due	**Literacy:** Partner storytelling (peer critique) **Writing:** Final drafts and publishing story What will exhibition look like? **Art:** Rocketship exhibition invitations	**Literacy:** Partner storytelling **Writing:** Final drafts and publishing story (soft deadline) **Exhibition practice:** What will it look like when we tell our constellation myths? **Blog Post:** Imagine yourself at exhibition, what will it be like?

WEEK EIGHT

Focus of the week: Exhibition practice & exhibition !

Exhibition practice: What will it look like when we are explaining our constellation and the tinkering behind it? 1. Organize inquiry journal and data collection 2. Practice questions guests will ask 3. Talk about order	**Exhibition practice:** Dress rehearsal for 6th graders - critique and reflection Continue any unfinished work!	**Exhibition practice:** Final dress rehearsal Last minute tips and feedback 6PM EXHIBITION!	**Project reflection day** 1. Whole group reflection: What was the most important thing you learned in The Story of the Stars project? 2. Small group reflection: Tell me about something you did well during this project. Tell me something that was challenging. 3. Self reflection page: tell about a time you collaborated during this project	

A DAY IN THE LIFE OF A STUDENT IN THIS PROJECT...

A day in the life of a student in this classroom starts with morning meeting, then literacy rotations, then math rotations, followed by writers' workshop, a dedicated time for projects and ends with an exploratory hour called "Tinkering" that focuses on art and engineering. This school focuses on three core practices: (1) Project Based Learning, (2) Social & Emotional Learning and (3) Blended Learning, using rotational model.

Not all teaching and learning during the project was executed in the context of the project. On average, 40-60% of each day was spent on learning and activities connected to the project context. Where it seemed natural, the project was incorporated into the daily routine. However some foundational skills necessary to kindergartners as well as learning outcomes unrelated to the project were taught out of context from the project.

Thus, the ratio between learning embedded in the project and foundational knowledge and skills taught out of the context of the project fluctuated throughout the eight week-long Story of the Stars project, depending on the needs of the students and the needs of the project.

WHAT IS PBL?

NUTS & BOLTS CRITERIA

	FULLY MET	PARTIALLY MET	NOT YET MET
ACADEMIC LEARNING OUTCOMES			
The project is focused on helping students meet and develop mastery of a reasonable scope of learning outcomes aligned to standards or programs of study in one or more subject areas or disciplines.			
21ST CENTURY COMPETENCIES			
The project incorporates the teaching and assessing of a targeted 21st Century Competency, such as collaboration, critical thinking, presentational communication and creativity.			
TANGIBLE OUTCOMES			
The project challenges students to develop high quality, portfolio-ready products, performances, presentations and/or services that are evidential of learning, useful beyond the classroom and exhibited to a relevant audience.			
FOCUSED INQUIRY			
The implementation of the project is modeled off of a method of inquiry used in the adult world such as the scientific method, the historical method, design thinking, the engineering design process, a process for problem solving, etc.			
FOCUSING QUESTION(S)			
Projects are initiated and focused with either an "essential question" that promotes enduring understandings and/or by a "driving question" – an open-ended, concrete, and easily understandable question that is motivating to students and answered by students at the end of the project through their tangible outcomes. Teachers and/or students can write focusing question(s).			
ENGAGING CONTEXT			
The project is grounded in a problem, controversy, scenario, simulation, current event, challenge or issue that is authentic, engaging and/or meaningful to students.			
STUDENT VOICE & CHOICE			
Students are given opportunities (depending on age and experience with PBL) to express (1) voice – their opinion, perspective, idea or answer in the distinctive style or tone of their choosing and (2) choice – selecting between two or more product options or making key decisions about how, when, where and with whom they will conduct project work.			
DRAFTING & CRITIQUE			
Throughout the project, students are given multiple opportunities to draft, revise, improve and refine their tangible outcomes with the use of structured opportunities for critique from multiple sources – self, peers, teacher and adults.			
ADULT WORLD CONNECTIONS			
At all stages of the project, students connect with the adult world through fieldwork, authentic documents and data and/or work with organizations, experts, stakeholders and professionals.			

PHASES OF PROJECT PLANNING

PHASE 1: Big Picture Planning

A. Select Learning Outcomes – What do you want students to know, be able to do and understand by the end of the project? Which standards, topics and concepts will be addressed by project work?

B. Contextualize Learning Outcomes – How will you anchor the content in an authentic context? Describe a problem, challenge, controversy, design challenge, tribute work challenge, issue or scenario that links your content to something real-world and relevant.

C. Craft Focusing Question(s) – Begin drafting an open-ended, motivating question that will be posed at the beginning of the project, that will focus the inquiry process and that will be answered by students at the end of the project through their products, performances, presentations or services.

D. Determine Tangible Outcomes – What products, presentations, performances and/or services will give students the opportunity to "show what they know" at the end of the project? How could they be authentic, e.g. useful to an outside audience?

E. Connect with the Adult World – Best-case scenario – who will work with students during the project and serve as an audience at the end of the project. These could be community members, stakeholders, experts, community organizations, clients, etc…

PHASE 2: Feedback & Revision

Share your work with colleagues and request feedback in the form of:

"I like…..because….." "I wonder…." "I suggest…."

Then, review feedback and make relevant revisions to your work.

PHASE 3: In-depth Planning

Continue developing your project by completing the following important planning forms:

A. Project Alignment Guide
B. Project Calendar
C. Project in a Nutshell

As you make progress, solicit feedback and use protocols, as needed. Then, return to developing and refining your project.

PHASE 4: Critique & Refinement

Conduct one or more Tuning Protocols (*see page 62*) with colleagues, and even students. Ideally, you would seek out in-depth feedback multiple times, and no later than one week prior to launching your project. Following the protocol(s), revise and refine your project. Remember, feedback is only useful if you use it. You can toggle back and forth between phases 3 and 4 until you feel ready to get started.

PHASE 1 – BIG PICTURE PLANNING
STEP 1 & 2: CONTENT & CONTEXT

Contextualize your learning outcomes in a meaningful, authentic and/or engaging way.

Use one or more of the following options to provide context:

1. National, international, local issues or current event
2. An authentic role
3. A controversy
4. A design, product or engineering challenge found in the workplace
5. An authentic problem
6. A premise or simulation that's authentic and/or genuinely interesting to students
7. Tribute Work

Summarize your context.   *List learning outcomes.*

CONTEXT	LEARNING OUTCOMES

 This can be a "chicken and egg" game. You can start with content and hunt and gather for an authentic context. Or you can select an anchor context and then hunt and gather for content. Your choice.

AUTHENTICITY CHECK	YES	NOT YET
Is the project anchored in a context that is real and would be meaningful to students?		
Is it a problem, question, controversy, current event, etc. that might actually be addressed by an adult at work or by members of the community?		

STEP 3: FOCUSING QUESTION(S)

Hook students and focus the inquiry process with one or more well-crafted focusing questions.

Essential questions are anchored in big ideas and concepts. They are used to promote the development of enduring understandings.

Driving questions are posed on the first day of a project, revisited frequently and answered by students at the end of a project in the form of their tangible products, presentations, performances or services.

Remember, questions should...
- be engaging, interesting & intriguing.
- be open-ended and therefore will elicit multiple possible "right answers."
- NOT be "Google-able."
- have a roll-off-the-tongue factor (avoid overly lengthy questions or challenging terms.)

INSTRUCTIONS: Draft a preliminary focusing question. Depending on your project, it will make sense to write either an essential question or a driving question. Write your initial idea in the draft section. Then, use the tips above to attempt to revise, improve and finalize your question below.

DRAFT	How can we use campfires to meet our needs?/ How do campfires meet our needs?
REVISED	
REVISED	
REVISED	
FINAL	

STEP 4: TANGIBLE OUTCOMES

What will students produce individually and in teams to show what they know and can do? Options include products, performances, presentations and/or services.

Remember: Well-designed projects…
- Balance both team and individual products.
- Integrate end products that mimic what real professionals produce in the real world.
- Should structure products that have an open-ended component – voice and/or choice.

INSTRUCTIONS: Determine what project-based outcomes students will produce throughout the project. List them in the applicable boxes below.

PRODUCTS
☐ Class   ☐ Team   ☐ Individual

PERFORMANCES
☐ Class   ☐ Team   ☐ Individual

PRESENTATIONS
☐ Class   ☐ Team   ☐ Individual

SERVICES
☐ Class   ☐ Team   ☐ Individual

Voice can be incorporated by allowing students to express, in the distinctive style or tone of their choosing, their opinions, perspectives, ideas, solutions and/or their unique answers to the focusing question.

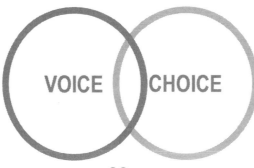

VOICE   CHOICE

Choice is can be given to students by allowing them to select between two or more product options. It can also be given by providing options in terms of how, when, where and with whom work is completed.

PHASE 1 – BIG PICTURE PLANNING

STEP 5: ADULT WORLD CONNECTIONS

Connect students and their project work to the adult world.

Adult World Connections can include:

- Organizations
- Community Members
- Industry Professionals
- Experts
- Stakeholders
- Authentic Data, Documents, Models & Texts
- Field Work, Primary Research, Experimentation, Data & Observations

 SUCCESS STORY: *On the second day of an Introduction to PBL workshop, a teacher cold-emailed a local business to see if she could rally some troops to participate in her project. She received a reply 14 minutes later. The business owner eagerly replied that they'd love to help! She laid out her requests and they solidified dates and commitments. Students later reported that having adult involvement in the project motivated them to produce higher quality work and raised the stakes for them personally. Lesson: Don't be afraid to reach out!*

ADULT WORLD CONNECTIONS		
Authentic Documents, Data, Samples and/or Models	Organizations, Experts, Stakeholders and/or Professionals	Primary Data, Surveys, Polls, Experimentation, Field Work and/or Direct Observations

FRAMING DESIGN CHALLENGES

FRAME THE DESIGN CHALLENGE:

_____

(Action Verb)

> Build, Create, Engineer, Craft, Draft, Plan, Invent, Construct, Develop, Conceptualize, Design, Prototype, Refine, Improve, etc.

_____

(Noun)

> State the thing that is being made or designed.

that_____

_____

_____

> Outline 2-5 design parameters. These often relate back to the targeted learning outcomes.

_____

for_____

> State purpose and/or audience.

DETERMINE MATERIALS:

List Materials

State whether this is an exhaustive list or a list one can add to.

STRUCTURE TEAMS:

Outline teaming parameters:

- Triads
- Individuals
- Pairs
- The Fantastic Four
- Flexible Grouping
- Other

OUTLINE ROLES:

Optional: If roles are being used, outline them.

SELECT PROCESSES:

Optional: Will you use the engineering design cycle, design thinking or some other method of inquiry to structure the process of the design challenge?

FRAMING DESIGN CHALLENGES

THE CHALLENGE:

MATERIALS:

TEAMS:

ROLES:

PROCESSES:

Find this free
resource at
www.pblconsulting.org

GALLERY WALK POSTER DRAFT

TITLE *(Should be cool, pithy catchy, and short)*	
GRADE LEVEL SUBJECT AREA	Pre-K
STEP 1: LEARNING OUTCOMES	Outdoor cooking Spatial awareness fire building natural elements risk managment Parent/community envirenment Sense of community Story telling/Songs/Dancing
STEP 2: CONTEXT *(Why would we need to know or care to know the content?)*	Campfires • transference of home life to school life • Connecting children to natural elements • Outdoor cooking * learning to meet basic needs thru natural resources + Community
STEP 3: FOCUSING QUESTION(S)	What can we do with a Campfire?
STEP 4: TANGIBLE OUTCOMES *(How will students show what they know and can do? Be sure to allow for voice & choice.)*	• cooking food - cook book • family campout - song/story book/audible CD Packing list • Building/setting up fire • Story telling/Sing Songs • Teachers of fire safety - fire safety booklet/presentation
STEP 5: ADULT WORLD CONNECTIONS	Oral traditions Park Ranger/Wildland fire fighter/ boy/girlscouts/NOLS Fire Rating/Permits Community cookbook Weather observations burn site visits woods fires

PHASE 2 – FEEDBACK & REVISION

REFLECTION ON FEEDBACK

GALLERY WALK PROTOCOL	TIME
SET-UP Hang posters and distribute sticky notes.	5 mins
GALLERY WALK & FEEDBACK Silently record feedback on sticky notes using specific "I likes" and "I wonders." Give at least one "I like" and one "I wonder" per poster.	15 mins
REFLECTION Reflect on the feedback for the purpose of revising and improving your work.	10 mins
TOTAL	30 mins

POST-GALLERY WALK REFLECTION		
	MAJOR / MINOR CHANGES	THINGS TO BE CONSIDERED OR INVESTIGATED
LEARNING OUTCOMES		
CONTEXT		
FOCUSING QUESTION(S)		
TANGIBLE OUTCOMES		
ADULT WORLD CONNECTIONS		

BRACKET CHALLENGE

INSTRUCTIONS: Pit the Nuts and Bolts against one another in this bracket challenge. Discuss matched pairs and reach consensus as you move winners forward in each bracket. Continue until you determine a bracket winner. Use the criteria on the Nuts and Bolts criteria to amp up the level of your discussion.

Consider this question as you discuss:

Which of the 9 Nuts and Bolts would help create the most powerful learning?

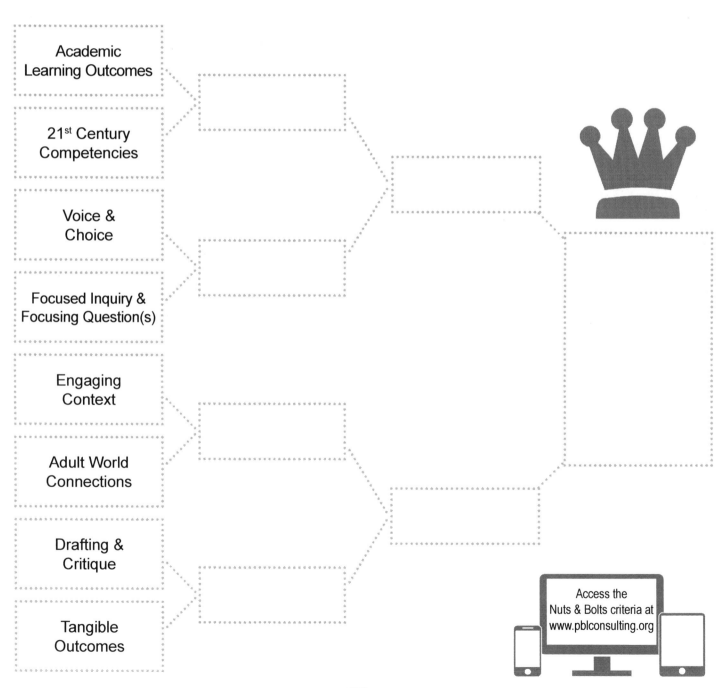

- Academic Learning Outcomes
- 21st Century Competencies
- Voice & Choice
- Focused Inquiry & Focusing Question(s)
- Engaging Context
- Adult World Connections
- Drafting & Critique
- Tangible Outcomes

Access the Nuts & Bolts criteria at www.pblconsulting.org

NUTS & BOLTS CRITERIA

	FULLY MET	PARTIALLY MET	NOT YET MET
ACADEMIC LEARNING OUTCOMES			
The project is focused on helping students meet and develop mastery of a reasonable scope of learning outcomes aligned to standards or programs of study in one or more subject areas or disciplines.			
21ST CENTURY COMPETENCIES			
The project incorporates the teaching and assessing of a targeted 21st Century Competency, such as collaboration, critical thinking, presentational communication and creativity.			
TANGIBLE OUTCOMES			
The project challenges students to develop high quality, portfolio-ready products, performances, presentations and/or services that are evidential of learning, useful beyond the classroom and exhibited to a relevant audience.			
FOCUSED INQUIRY			
The implementation of the project is modeled off of a method of inquiry used in the adult world such as the scientific method, the historical method, design thinking, the engineering design process, a process for problem solving, etc.			
FOCUSING QUESTION(S)			
Projects are initiated and focused with either an "essential question" that promotes enduring understandings and/or by a "driving question" – an open-ended, concrete, and easily understandable question that is motivating to students and answered by students at the end of the project through their tangible outcomes. Teachers and/or students can write focusing question(s).			
ENGAGING CONTEXT			
The project is grounded in a problem, controversy, scenario, simulation, current event, challenge or issue that is authentic, engaging and/or meaningful to students.			
STUDENT VOICE & CHOICE			
Students are given opportunities (depending on age and experience with PBL) to express (1) voice – their opinion, perspective, idea or answer in the distinctive style or tone of their choosing and (2) choice – selecting between two or more product options or making key decisions about how, when, where and with whom they will conduct project work.			
DRAFTING & CRITIQUE			
Throughout the project, students are given multiple opportunities to draft, revise, improve and refine their tangible outcomes with the use of structured opportunities for critique from multiple sources – self, peers, teacher and adults.			
ADULT WORLD CONNECTIONS			
At all stages of the project, students connect with the adult world through fieldwork, authentic documents and data and/or work with organizations, experts, stakeholders and professionals.			

PHASE 3 – IN-DEPTH PLANNING
PROJECT PLANNING CHECKLIST

INSTRUCTIONS: Use these checklists to monitor work completion during the project design process.

DESIGNING THE PROJECT	✔	TO DO	?
I have selected a clear scope of learning outcomes aligned to my curriculum and/or standards documents.			
I have contextualized the learning outcomes in an engaging way with a problem, scenario, challenge, current event, controversy, issue, etc.			
I have drafted and refined my focusing question(s).			
I have determined the tangible outcomes through which students will "show what they know," with reasonable opportunities for voice and choice. These tangible outcomes are aligned to learning outcomes within the determined scope and will allow me to see evidence of student learning.			
I have delineated between individual and team assignments, tasks & products.			
I have envisioned adult world connections – field work, observations, primary data, work with authentic documents and data, work with organizations, professionals, stakeholders etc.			
I have used the Nuts & Bolts criteria or other key criteria to assess my project in development.			
I have solicited feedback from peers, colleagues, students and/or experts and used that feedback to revise, refine and reflect on my project-in-development.			

 META MOMENT: The first day of the Intro to PBL workshop is structured in a way that prompts you to make substantial progress on all of the steps and tasks outlined above in the "Designing the Project" checklist.

How could you scaffold and structure the process of your project so that students are inherently prompted to meet the requirements, make sufficient progress and achieve great outcomes?

PROJECT PLANNING CHECKLIST

INSTRUCTIONS: Use these checklists to monitor work completion during the project design process.

CREATING AN ASSESSMENT PLAN	✔	TO DO	?
I have completed the Project Alignment Guide to align tangible outcomes, learning outcomes, instruction and assessment.			
I have built in opportunities and structures for drafting and critique during the project that involves self, peers, teachers and/or experts.			
I have selected and/or developed reflection prompts to be used during and at the end of the project regarding content and process.			
I have targeted a key 21st Century Competency to teach and assess. It is included in my Project Alignment Guide.			
I have designed or selected rubrics that are aligned to my learning outcomes to measure student learning through tangible outcomes both formatively and summatively.			

PREPARING TO LAUNCH AND MANAGE THE PROCESS	✔	TO DO	?
I have developed an engaging launch activity that (1) creates purpose, (2) launches inquiry and (3) paints a clear picture of the end in mind.			
I have completed my project calendar with weekly focuses and possibly daily snapshots.			
Optional: I have developed team rosters or a teaming strategy.			
Optional: I have decided which roles students may assume during the project.			
Optional: I have created a resource bank for students to guide inquiry and to support project work.			
I have determined how and when to integrate various technologies.			
I have collected and/or created forms, logs, graphic organizers, tools and handouts that can be used throughout the project.			

PROJECT ALIGNMENT GUIDE

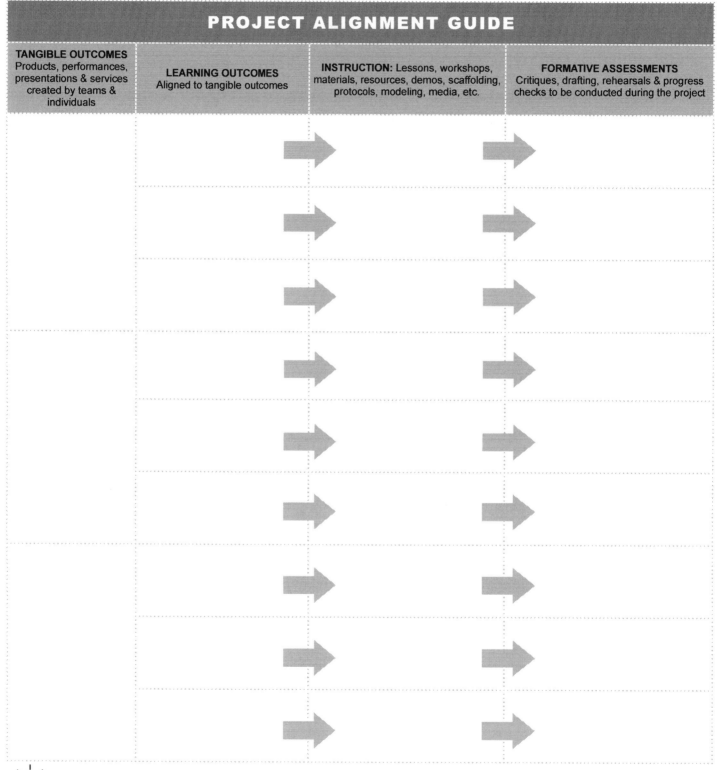

PROJECT ALIGNMENT GUIDE			
TANGIBLE OUTCOMES Products, performances, presentations & services created by teams & individuals	**LEARNING OUTCOMES** Aligned to tangible outcomes	**INSTRUCTION:** Lessons, workshops, materials, resources, demos, scaffolding, protocols, modeling, media, etc.	**FORMATIVE ASSESSMENTS** Critiques, drafting, rehearsals & progress checks to be conducted during the project

TIP: Use this Project Alignment Guide template to align tangible outcomes, learning outcomes, instruction and assessment for your project. Use the examples in the sample project section of the workbook and on the web to guide your work.

Find this free resource at www.pblconsulting.org

MY LEARNING AND WORK PLAN

 META MOMENT: Project Based Learning frequently integrates instructional components (mini-workshops, lectures, videos, readings, texts, lessons, etc.) that are offered both optionally and/or on demand to students. Instructional offerings are aligned to student "need to knows" as the inquiry process progresses.

OPTIONAL MINI-SESSIONS	RSVP		OPT-OUT WORK PLAN
	YES	NO (Indicate work plan & deliverable)	
Time: _____ Mini-Workshop: **Inquiry in PBL**			
Time: _____ Mini-Workshop: **Teaching & Assessing 21st Century Competencies**			
Time: _____ Mini-Workshop: **Drafting & Critique**			

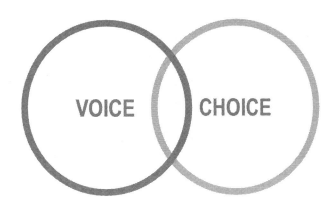

INQUIRY IN PBL

METHODS OF FOCUSED INQUIRY

These two methods of inquiry are fairly similar. They are used in the adult world by designers and by engineers to conceptualize, plan, create and improve new "things" that have value.

Increasingly, teachers, students and schools at all levels are using these methods, which are already common in industry, to frame a process for making and creating.

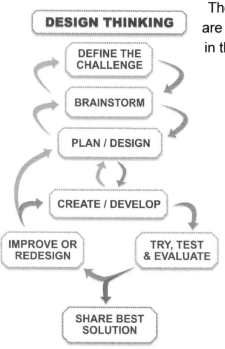

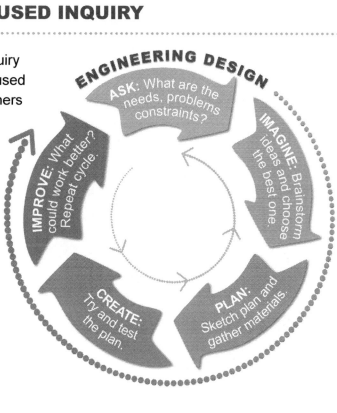

Generally speaking, the Engineering Design Cycle is used to create structures, systems, machines, engines & code. Design Thinking handles everything else.

The Historical Method is used by historians to write new accurate accounts of the past.

The purpose of the Scientific Method is to discover "new truths" about the natural world.

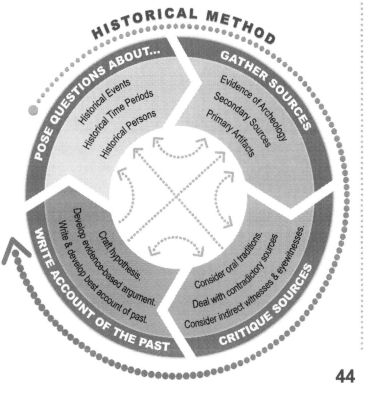

THE SCIENTIFIC METHOD

OBSERVE, QUESTION, WONDER
Look at the world around you. Why are things the way they are?

TRY TO EXPLAIN...
Interpret your observations and conduct preliminary research.

CRAFT HYPOTHESIS
If you can't explain your observations, develop a possible explanation.

TEST HYPOTHESIS
Design and carry out an experiment

INTERPRET RESULTS
Make sense of observations and collected data from experiment

REPORT FINDINGS
Draw and share conclusions to whom they matter.

INQUIRY DEFINED: Attempting to resolve that which is unresolved, using a process.

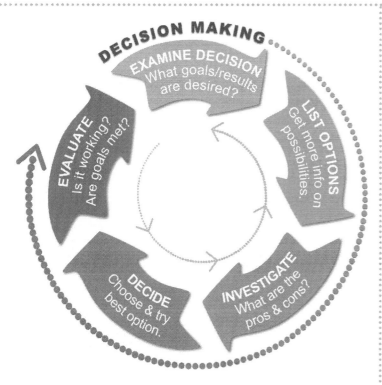

We all make decisions on a daily basis, but rarely do we carefully use a decision making process, like this one. Imagine the world we'd live in if we all did!

This process is most often used in the fields of politics, business, marketing, military strategy and more.

As the pattern reveals, many of these methods are used within specific disciplinary domains. Open-ended inquiry is "non-discipline specific" method. It could also be called "Generic Inquiry." Using this method is a great option if your project doesn't ask learners to take on an "adult-world professional role." E.g. Acting like a historian, scientist or engineer.

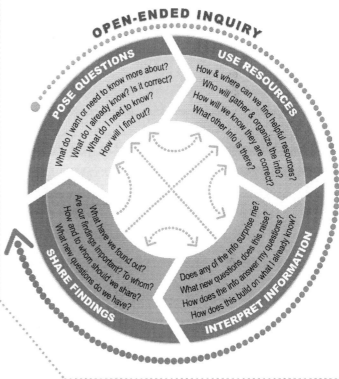

Other than "open-ended inquiry," this problem solving process may be the most "disciplinarily-neutral" method available. Just think, there is no and seemingly never will be a shortage of real-world problems.

This is true in every thinkable discipline and domain. John Dewey even posited that, "we only think when we are confronted with problems." As a pragmatist, he believed the goal of thinking was to guide how to act well within our world and lives.

Find these free graphics & journals at www.pblconsulting.org

MINI-WORKSHOP

21st CENTURY COMPETENCIES

PURPOSE: To define 21st Century Competencies and to determine how I will teach and assess one or more competencies in my project.

Teaching & Assessing 21st Century Competencies

	WHAT IS IT?	HOW WILL I TEACH IT?	HOW WILL I ASSESS IT?
CRITICAL THINKING			
COLLABORATION			
CREATIVITY & INNOVATION			
PRESENTATION			

INSTRUCTIONS: Indicate which 21st Century Competency you will teach and assess during your project in the star above.

INSTRUCTIONS: Review the protocols on the following pages and answer the questions below to determine how, when and where to integrate various opportunities for drafting and critique into your project as well as to select the best processes to structure the process of drafting and critique.

WHAT TYPES OF WORK-IN-PROGRESS AND DRAFTS OF TANGIBLE OUTCOMES WILL EMERGE DURING THE PROJECT?

WHICH PROTOCOLS WILL YOU USE TO STRUCTURE THE PROCESS OF TUNING DRAFTS OF TANGIBLE OUTCOMES?

HOW WILL YOU INVOLVE SELF, PEERS, TEACHERS AND EXPERTS INTO THE PROCESS OF DRAFTING & CRITIQUE?

FRAME PROMPTS & QUESTIONS FOR REFLECTION AND SELF ASSESSMENT OF DRAFTS AND WORK-IN-PROGRESS

OTHER CONSIDERATIONS?

 NEXT STEP: Input your plans for drafting and critique - tuning, formative assessment and reflection - into your Project Alignment Guide.

DRAFTING & CRITIQUE

WHACK-A-MOLE PROTOCOL

Place student work, along with criteria, critique instructions and/or questions for reflection, at student desks and/or stations. Students move around as space is available to participate in the critique for multiple pieces of work. The idea is that they pop up when they finish each critique,like a mole in the "Whack-A-Mole" game. Then, they pop back down in a new spot to conduct another critique, wherever one is available. This works well when the time it will take to conduct critique will predictably vary.

CHARETTE PROTOCOL

This protocol was typically used in engineering. It is best used early on to feed-forward, rather than back. As soon as a process stalls, students can call a "charette" to get fresh perspectives and ideas on how to move their project forward.

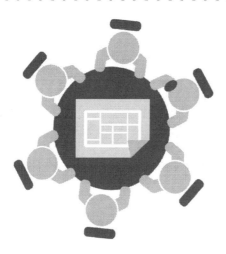

PAIR CRITIQUE

Students are paired with a critique partner. Pairs respond directly to critique and feedback questions generated by the teachers, the class and/or by the work author or designer.

EXIT SLIPS

Prepared in advance by the teacher or done on-the-fly, exit slips can act as a check for understanding and/or collect information on work completion, effectiveness of instruction, process, materials, and more.

2 STARS & A WISH

Students can acknowledge and share 2 things that were done well. Then they share a wish they have that would enhance the work being examined.

Find these free resources at www.pblconsulting.org

DRAFTING & CRITIQUE

GALLERY WALK

Text-lite work is hung in a space to mimic a"gallery." Participants walk the gallery and offer written feedback (often on Post-It Notes) in response to a prompt and/or using generic critique language.

INSTRUCTIONAL CRITIQUE

The teacher (or students) lead a small group or the whole class in the critique of one or more work samples to distill the quality indicators of said work. E.g. Thesis statements. The indicators can then be used to assess the students' work in progress. E.g. Students' draft thesis statements.

DILEMMA PROTOCOL

Student(s) present a dilemma, e.g. getting stuck, encountering a tricky problem, writer's block, etc. and protocol participants offer constructive feedback about how to respond to the dilemma.

ABC OF A TEXT

Create a acronym, each letter asks students to look for something specific in the work being examined.
e.g. SLUG

    S - Spelling

    L - Letter Formation

    U - Uppercase (first letter of first word in sentence)

    G - Greatness (what's great about the work)

OBJECTIVE: I can plan & schedule instruction to prompt reflection and involve students in assessment. (e.g. co-create rubrics/criteria, unpack criteria, name levels of performances, defining the process, instructional critique protocols, etc.)

FISHBOWL

The protocol uses two concentric circles to create an inner circle and an outer circle. The protocol can be used for discussion or reflection. Those seated in the inner circle discuss a topic or prompt and those seated in the outer circle listen, observe, take notes or complete other designated tasks. Often an empty seat is placed in the inner circle. This "hot seat" modification can allow multiple outer circle participants to join the inner circle discussion temporarily.

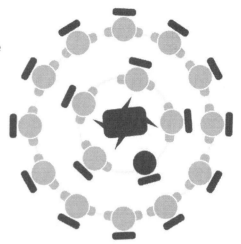

3, 2, 1

You can write any 3 questions or prompts. Students provide 3 responses to the first, 2 to the second and one to the final. Usually the first question or prompt is easier and lends itself to multiple responses and the final question or prompt is more complex.

CHALK TALK

In this protocol, a word, phrase, question or prompt is written on a chalk board, white board, butcher paper, etc. In silence, students approach the board and respond in writing. Their responses can connect to the initial prompt or they can connect directly to other responses. Multiple students can respond simultaneously. Students can respond multiple times. It ends when it ends. The entire protocol is silent.

SUCCESS ANALYSIS PROTOCOL

This protocol is all about determining cause and effect. When someone experiences a profound success, this protocol can help uncover that which led to the success. i.e. cause and effect. The idea is that through the identification and analysis of causal factors, promoting subsequent "successes" will be more likely. Learn more about this protocol on www.nrsfharmony.org

 OBJECTIVE: I can plan & schedule instruction to involve students in assessment, to teach how to conduct high quality assessment and to prompt reflection.

Find these free resources at www.pblconsulting.org

DRAFTING & CRITIQUE

WORLD CAFE

In this protocol for discussion, each table is assigned a topic, with a discussion prompt. Participants select the table and topic of their choice and discuss the topic and prompt for 5-10 minutes. Participants switch tables 3-4 times, selecting their top topics. It can feel a bit like "musical chairs," but with enough rotations, one usually gets their top choices of topics by the end. At each table, using chart or butcher paper, groups attempt to create a visual representation of their discussion, with minimal usage of words. Groups review and build on previous discussion visuals and share their final one.

CONTINUUM DIALOG

This protocol could be adapted to be used with students for discussion or reflection. In this protocol, an affirmative and negative statement are posed. Participants physically stand on a continuum. The continuum is indicated physically in the room as an arc in order for all participants to see where others place themselves. Placement on the continuum reveals participants' positions in regards to the posed statements. Once participants have placed themselves on the continuum the facilitator can ask them to explain (2 mins or less) why they placed themselves where they did. No rebuttals, no arguments, no judgment.

As participants listen and hear different perspectives, they can physically move themselves in the event that their perspective shifts.

Learn more about how to facilitate this protocol at www.nrsfharmony.org

QUESTIONS FOR REFLECTION

Common questions could include:

1. What have you learned from doing this project?

Content	Process

2. On a scale of 1-4, how difficult was this project? Explain...
3. What have you learned about yourself?

As A Learner	As A Team Member

4. What would you do differently in future projects and why?

CRAFTING AN ENTRY EVENT

PURPOSE: To develop an entry event for your project that will generate interest, curiosity, motivation and a need to know.

TYPES OF ENTRY EVENTS

- Letters requesting assistance
- Memos
- Field trips / field work
- Demos
- Skits
- Video montages
- Provocative issues
- Startling statistics
- Case studies
- Guest speakers
- Documentaries

PURPOSE OF ENTRY EVENTS

- Call to action
- Connect to purpose
- Create a need to know
- Connect to end in mind
- Prompt students to ask questions about:
  1. Process
  2. Products
  3. Content
- Generate motivation, curiosity & interest
- To *genuinely engage* students

ENTRY EVENTS SHOULD NOT...

Feel like an assignment...   Feel like more work...   Leave students confused...

CONCEPTUALIZE YOUR ENTRY EVENT HERE...

COMMON TEAM ROLES

Below are some common team roles used in projects from grades 4-12. They can be written and treated like job descriptions.

TEAM LEADER

- Establishes and runs team meetings
- Sets and monitors goals & agreements and redirects team, as needed
- Delegates tasks and divides work, as needed
- Mediates conflict between team members
- Encourager

Key Trait:
Relationship-oriented

RESEARCH LEAD

- Goes outside of provided materials to gather and share useful information.
- Focuses on "supporting on the sidelines"
- Helps team overcome obstacles and roadblocks.
- Collects, maintains and uses the Team Need to Know List to drive work

Key Trait:
Resourceful

ORGANIZATIONAL LEAD

- Keeps time during activities and phases of design
- Maintains a schedules and tracks progress toward goals and milestones
- Keeps track of materials
- Organizes and maintains team documents

Key Trait:
Detail-oriented

DESIGN LEAD

- Directs team to use the design process.
- Tracks team's use of each phase of design
- Gathers team perspectives, makes key design decisions

Key Trait:
Process-oriented

ARCHIVIST

- Archives team's work in progress, drafts and prototypes
- Takes photos and videos of work in progress
- Captures quotes, moments & process

Key Trait:
Reflective

CURATOR

- Focuses on how work will be displayed at the end
- Pays attention to detail without losing sight of the big picture
- Collaborates with other curators to ensure continuity of work curating at the end
- Consults with team on during project

Key Trait:
Visionary

In addition to these "generic" roles, ask yourself: "If I was a professional in industry creating a comparable tangible outcome to the students in this project, what would my job be? What would my title be? What would some of the key elements of my job description be?" Could the answers to those questions help you frame a role for your specific project?

Professional Title:

Job Description: **Key Duties:**

SECONDARY SAMPLE CONTRACT

TEAM AGREEMENT

ROLES & RESPONSIBILITIES

Which roles will team members take on? What responsibilities will they have?	What are they the best fit for this role? What strengths do they bring?

How will your team support team members when they have excused or unexcused absences?

COMMUNICATION

What are our norms for discussion and communication?

How will we collaborate when we are not meeting in person? E.g. File sharing, real-time collaboration, project management system, etc.

How will we conduct team meetings? How often?

How will we make decisions? How will we resolve conflict?

Just like in the adult world, team members can be fired during a project. What would justify a firing? What steps would be taken prior to a firing?

SECONDARY SAMPLE CONTRACT

TEAM AGREEMENT			
TASKS & MILESTONES	**DUE DATE**	**LEAD**	**TASK STATUS**

ADDITIONAL AGREEMENTS

PRINTED NAMES, SIGNATURES & DATE

Find this free
resource at
www.pblconsulting.org

ELEMENTARY SAMPLE CONTRACT A

TEAM AGREEMENT

Team Name: _____   Project: _____

BEING A TEAM MEMBER

| My name is _____ and I will help with the project by... | My name is _____ and I will help with the project by... | My name is _____ and I will help with the project by... |

TALKING AS A TEAM

| When we speak to each other, we... | If someone misses something, we will... | We will meet on... |

WORKING AS A TEAM

| When we don't agree, we... | If someone misses something, we will... | We will meet on... |

ELEMENTARY SAMPLE CONTRACT B

TEAM AGREEMENT

Team Name: _____   Project: _____

BEING A TEAM MEMBER

My name is _____
and I will help with the project by...

My name is _____
and I will help with the project by...

My name is _____
and I will help with the project by...

TALKING AS A TEAM

When we speak to each other, we...

When we make decisions, we...

WORKING AS A TEAM

When we don't agree, we.....

If someone misses something, we will....

Find these free
resources at
www.pblconsulting.org

STRUCTURING THE CALENDAR

The flow of an elementary project models the phases of inquiry.

While every project rolls out differently based on the nature of the learning, the style of the teacher the needs of the learners and more, the following shares general trends at each phase of the project.

FLOW OF AN ELEMENTARY PROJECT

PHASE ONE - FIRST 10-25% OF THE PROJECT

PHASE ONE FOCUS: In this phase the focus is on launching the project and building background knowledge. Sometimes, a singular entry event is insufficient, particularly in the lower elementary grades. Frequently, teachers revisit the "why" and the "what" behind the project multiple times in the first days and weeks. The goal is to capture students' interest and help students generate questions. The teacher uses these questions, curiousities and wonders as a spring board for instruction that builds general background knowledge.

PHASE TWO - NEXT 15-40% OF THE PROJECT

PHASE TWO FOCUS: The focus now shifts to organizing work on tangible outcomes and, as needed, forming teams. If your project incorporates a lot of voice and choice, students' work on tangible outcomes may begin to go in different directions at this point. So, it's important to plan to support different paths of focused, in-depth inquiry to support learners as they work on their tangible outcomes.

PHASE THREE - NEXT 15-40% OF THE PROJECT

PHASE THREE FOCUS: Drafting and critique of tangible outcomes is the focus of this phase, in addition to continued in-depth and focused inquiry. Students have been applying their knowledge, skills and understandings to the development of their tangible outcomes. Now, the teacher should focus on structuring opportunities for learners to receive feedback and critique from multiple sources - self, peer, expert and teacher. Learners can use this feedback and critique to revise and refine their work in progress.

PHASE FOUR - FINAL 10-25% OF THE PROJECT

PHASE FOUR FOCUS: Finally, students prepare to share their tangible outcomes. The project culminates in an exhibition of student work and often "presentations of learning" to an authentic audience. Exhibition is followed by reflections by: the teacher, the whole class, individual learners, teams and maybe even experts and volunteers. Reflections may focus on one or more of the following: (1) the project, (2) the process and (3) ourselves as learners.

Be sure to end with a celebration!

 TIP: Although tempting, it's important *not* to "front-load" content prior to launching the project. The project *is* the context in which instruction and learning takes place. The project creates a "Need to Know" (or what we might call a "Care to Know") the content. This makes any instruction more relevant and the learning taking place so much more powerful.

STRUCTURING THE CALENDAR

These common practices and tips create a skeletal structure for the typical roll-out of a project at the secondary level. As you develop your calendar, put the "meat" from your Project Alignment Guide onto the "bones" (common practices) of the calendar.

COMMON PRACTICES AND TIPS FOR A SECONDARY PROJECT

PHASE ONE - FIRST 10-25% OF THE PROJECT

Getting started: Entry event "Need to Knows" Form teams Team contracts	Assess models, exemplars or samples to paint a picture of the end in mind.	Building background knowledge using a variety of methods.	Consider building in "Flex Days" to be responsive to formative assessments.	Build in checkpoint assessments.

PHASE TWO - NEXT 15-40% OF THE PROJECT

Begin ideation early.	Check in with learner "Need to Knows" often.	Consider building in "Flex Days" to be responsive to formative assessments.	Request drafts of tangible outcomes as key project benchmarks.	Be sure to support 21st Century Competency development.

PHASE THREE - NEXT 15-40% OF THE PROJECT

Facilitate "instructional critique" as a way of teaching.	Consider building in "Flex Days" to be responsive to formative assessments.	Provide multiple opportunities for formative assessment.	Structure critique protocols involving peers and experts.	Assess tangible outcomes against criteria, models, exemplars or samples.

PHASE FOUR - FINAL 10-25% OF THE PROJECT

Prepare for exhibitions.	Rehearse presentations of learning. Portfolio additions.	Rehearse presentations of learning. Portfolio additions.	Exhibition preparations.	Reflection on project. Celebration! Finalize portfolio additions.

 TIP: Use Post It Notes early on to develop your calendar so that you can flex and change elements easily.

PHASE 3 – IN-DEPTH PLANNING
PROJECT CALENDAR TEMPLATE

PROJECT CALENDAR

Project Title: | Focusing Question

WEEK ONE

Focus of the week:

WEEK TWO

Focus of the week:

WEEK THREE

Focus of the week:

WEEK FOUR

Focus of the week:

Find these free templates at
www.pblconsulting.org

PROJECT IN A NUTSHELL	
Project Title:	Estimated Length:
Subject(s):	Grade Level(s):

LEARNING OUTCOMES

Academic Learning Outcomes	21st Century Competencies
	☐ Collaboration ☐ Presentation ☐ Creativity & Innovation ☐ Critical Thinking ☐ Other:

ENGAGING CONTEXT

Type of project	Summary of the challenge, problem, controversy, issue, simulation...
☐ Design challenge ☐ Tribute work ☐ Problem solving ☐ Addressing a controversial issue ☐ Addressing a local / national / intl issue ☐ Simulation or scenario ☐ Other:	

FOCUSED INQUIRY

Focusing Question(s)	Method of inquiry to be used	Tools needed
	☐ Engineering Design Process ☐ Design Thinking ☐ Problem Solving Process ☐ Scientific Method ☐ Open Ended Inquiry ☐ Decision Making Process ☐ Historical Method ☐ Other:	☐ Inquiry Journals ☐ Reflection Prompts ☐ Observation ☐ Authentic Documents ☐ Primary Data ☐ Field Work ☐ Adults Outside of School ☐ Other:

TANGIBLE OUTCOMES: PRODUCTS, PERFORMANCES, PRESENTATIONS & SERVICES

Individual	Team	Class

ADULT WORLD CONNECTIONS

Authentic documents, data, samples, models, etc.	Professionals, stakeholders, organizations, experts, etc.	Primary research, field work, observation, experimentation

PHASE 4 - CRITIQUE & REFINEMENT
TUNING PROTOCOL

TUNING PROTOCOL	TIME
SHARING YOUR WORK Presenters explain their project; Audience listens and takes notes.	8 mins
CLARIFICATION Audience asks short clarifying questions; Presenters respond.	3 mins
THINK TIME Audience quietly thinks about what was shared. They may use criteria, such as the Nuts and Bolts Checklist, to guide their thinking about the project and to generate additional feedback. Presenters can use this time to quietly self assess.	3 mins
"I LIKE... BECAUSE..." Audience shares what they liked and why. Presenters listen and take notes.	4 mins
"I WONDER..." Audience shares concerns and questions for consideration. Presenters listen & take notes.	4 mins
"I SUGGEST..." Audience shares ideas & resources for the project. Presenters listen and take notes.	4 mins
REFLECTION Presenters share with audience what was helpful, useful and positive. Audience listens. Optionally, presenters may take a moment to reflect silently on useful feedback.	4 mins
TOTAL	30 mins

TUNING PROTOCOL MASTER SCHEDULE

ROUND	TIME & LOCATION	YOUR ROLE		
1		☐ Audience	☐ Facilitator	☐ Presenter
2		☐ Audience	☐ Facilitator	☐ Presenter
3		☐ Audience	☐ Facilitator	☐ Presenter
4		☐ Audience	☐ Facilitator	☐ Presenter
5		☐ Audience	☐ Facilitator	☐ Presenter

PREPARE TO SHARE

TITLE **GRADE LEVEL** **SUBJECT AREA** **LENGTH**	
FOCUSING QUESTION(S)	
ACADEMIC LEARNING OUTCOMES	
21ST CENTURY COMPETENCIES	
ENGAGING CONTEXT	
TANGIBLE OUTCOMES	
VOICE & CHOICE	
DRAFTING & CRITIQUE	
METHOD OF INQUIRY	
ADULT WORLD CONNECTIONS	
WHAT I LOVE ABOUT MY PROJECT	
THINGS I'D LIKE HELP WITH FOR MY PROJECT	

Find these free templates at www.pblconsulting.org

PHASE 4 - CRITIQUE & REFINEMENT

AUDIENCE NOTE TAKING GUIDE

	NOTES	LIKES	WONDERS	SUGGESTS
TITLE GRADE LEVEL SUBJECT AREA LENGTH				
FOCUSING QUESTION(S)				
ACADEMIC LEARNING OUTCOMES				
21ST CENTURY COMPETENCIES				
ENGAGING CONTEXT				
TANGIBLE OUTCOMES				
VOICE & CHOICE				
DRAFTING & CRITIQUE				
METHOD OF INQUIRY				
ADULT WORLD CONNECTIONS				
WHAT THEY LOVE ABOUT THE PROJECT				
WHAT THEY'D LIKE HELP ON THE PROJECT				

AUDIENCE NOTE TAKING GUIDE

	NOTES	LIKES	WONDERS	SUGGESTS
TITLE GRADE LEVEL SUBJECT AREA LENGTH				
FOCUSING QUESTION(S)				
ACADEMIC LEARNING OUTCOMES				
21ST CENTURY COMPETENCIES				
ENGAGING CONTEXT				
TANGIBLE OUTCOMES				
VOICE & CHOICE				
DRAFTING & CRITIQUE				
METHOD OF INQUIRY				
ADULT WORLD CONNECTIONS				
WHAT THEY LOVE ABOUT THE PROJECT				
WHAT THEY'D LIKE HELP ON THE PROJECT				

Find these free templates at www.pblconsulting.org

PHASE 4 - CRITIQUE & REFINEMENT
AUDIENCE NOTE TAKING GUIDE

	NOTES	LIKES	WONDERS	SUGGESTS
TITLE GRADE LEVEL SUBJECT AREA LENGTH				
FOCUSING QUESTION(S)				
ACADEMIC LEARNING OUTCOMES				
21ST CENTURY COMPETENCIES				
ENGAGING CONTEXT				
TANGIBLE OUTCOMES				
VOICE & CHOICE				
DRAFTING & CRITIQUE				
METHOD OF INQUIRY				
ADULT WORLD CONNECTIONS				
WHAT THEY LOVE ABOUT THE PROJECT				
WHAT THEY'D LIKE HELP ON THE PROJECT				

AUDIENCE NOTE TAKING GUIDE

	NOTES	LIKES	WONDERS	SUGGESTS
TITLE GRADE LEVEL SUBJECT AREA LENGTH				
FOCUSING QUESTION(S)				
ACADEMIC LEARNING OUTCOMES				
21ST CENTURY COMPETENCIES				
ENGAGING CONTEXT				
TANGIBLE OUTCOMES				
VOICE & CHOICE				
DRAFTING & CRITIQUE				
METHOD OF INQUIRY				
ADULT WORLD CONNECTIONS				
WHAT THEY LOVE ABOUT THE PROJECT				
WHAT THEY'D LIKE HELP ON THE PROJECT				

Find these free templates at www.pblconsulting.org

PHASE 4 - CRITIQUE & REFINEMENT

AUDIENCE NOTE TAKING GUIDE

	NOTES	LIKES	WONDERS	SUGGESTS
TITLE GRADE LEVEL SUBJECT AREA LENGTH				
FOCUSING QUESTION(S)				
ACADEMIC LEARNING OUTCOMES				
21ST CENTURY COMPETENCIES				
ENGAGING CONTEXT				
TANGIBLE OUTCOMES				
VOICE & CHOICE				
DRAFTING & CRITIQUE				
METHOD OF INQUIRY				
ADULT WORLD CONNECTIONS				
WHAT THEY LOVE ABOUT THE PROJECT				
WHAT THEY'D LIKE HELP ON THE PROJECT				

Find these free templates at www.pblconsulting.org

PHASE 4 - CRITIQUE & REFINEMENT
PRESENTER NOTE TAKING GUIDE

NOTES		
LIKES	**WONDERS**	**SUGGESTS**

REFLECTION - 3, 2, 1		
3 NEXT STEPS	**2 THINGS TO RECONSIDER**	**1 KEY CHANGE**

NOTES

Made in the USA
San Bernardino, CA
11 July 2017